To

My Parents for

Joy in Success,

Compassion in my fallibility,

Encouragement in my Academic Pursuits,

Understanding in my mistakes,

Support when my step falter,

And above all for making me what I am.

Preface

I have derived immense enthusiasm to write this book, titled, *Pandemic:In short,* from the encouragement I received from my parents and friends. I have tried to provide essential material. I have excluded certain unnecessary details.

The objective of writing this short book is to upgrade knowledge about the history of pandemics till update. As Noval corona virus (COVID 19) is on high peak these days and whole world is facing crisis.

Dr Sumit Singh Raina.

A pandemic is a scourge happening on a scale that crosses universal limits, generally influencing an enormous number of people. Pandemics can also happen in significant rural organisms (animals, crop plants, fish, tree species) or in different organisms. A sickness or condition is certainly not a pandemic just in light of the fact that it is boundless or executes numerous people; it should also be irresistible.

The World Health Organization (WHO) recently applied a six-arrange grouping that depicts the procedure by which a novel influenza virus moves from the first few infections in quite a while through to a pandemic. This beginnings with the virus for the most part contaminating creatures, with a few situations where creatures taint people, at that point moves through the phase where the virus starts to spread legitimately among people and finishes with a pandemic when infections from the new virus have spread around the world. In February 2020, WHO explained that "there is no official classification (for a pandemic)... For explanation, WHO doesn't utilize the old arrangement of 6 stages—that went from stage 1 (no reports of creature influenza prompting human infections) to stage 6 (a pandemic)—that a few people might be comfortable with from H1N1 2009.

HISTORY OF **PANDEMICS**

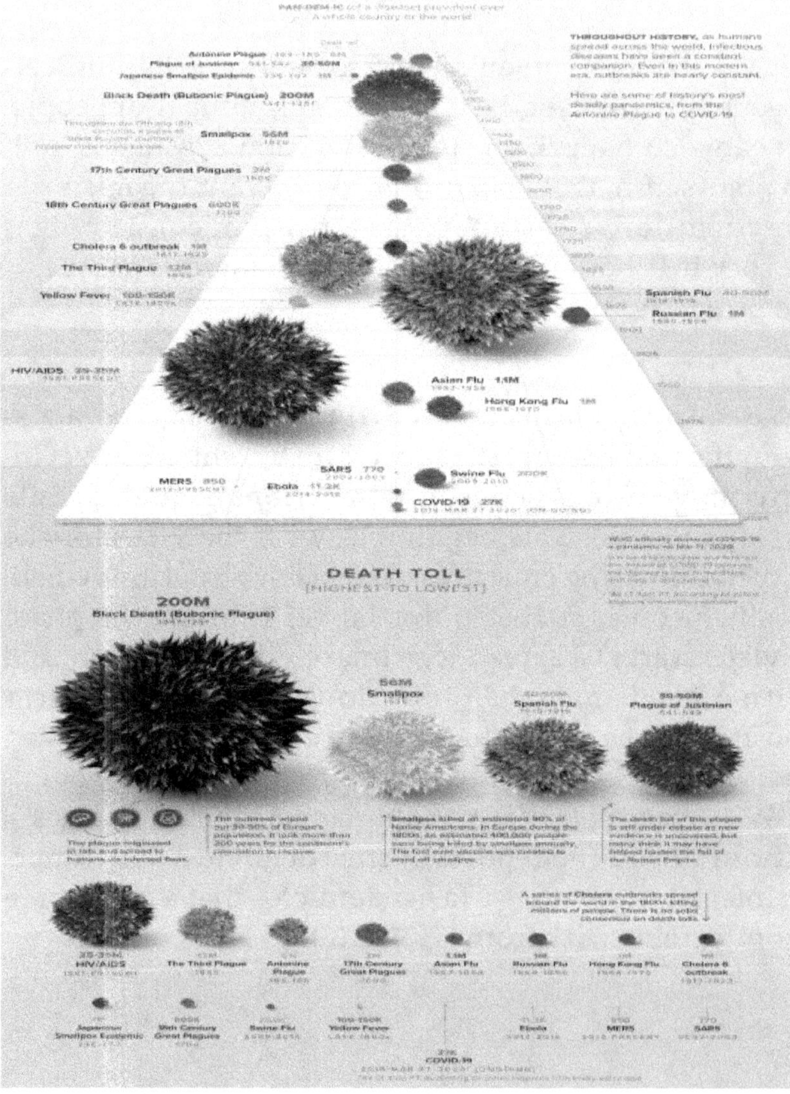

<u>Here are 20 of the worst Epidemics and Pandemics, dating from Prehistoric to Modern Times</u>

S.NO.	PANDEMICS & EPIDEMICS	TIME PERIOD
1.	Pre-Historic Epidemic	Circa 3000 B.C.
2.	Plague of Athens	430 B.C.
3.	Antonine Plague	165-180 B.C.
4.	Plague of Justinian	541-542 A.D.
5.	The Black Death	1346-1353
6.	Cocoliztli Epidemic	1545-1548
7.	American Plagues	16th Century
8.	Great Plague of London	1665-1666
9.	Great Plague of Marseille	1720-1723
10.	Russian Plague	1770-1772
11.	Philadelphia yellow Fever Epidemic	1793
12.	Flu Pandemic	1889-1890
13.	American Polio Epidemic	1916
14.	Spanish Flu	1918-1920
15.	Asian Flu	1957-1958
16.	AIDS Pandemic & Epidemic	1981-present day
17.	H1N1 Swine Flu	2009-10
18.	West African Ebola Epidemic	2014-16
19.	Zika Virus Epidemic	2015-Present day
20.	Novel Corona virus	2020

PRE-HISTORIC EPIDEMIC (CIRCA 3000B.C.)

Around 5,000 years back, an epidemic cleared out a prehistoric town in China. The assortments of the dead were full inside a house that was later burned to the ground. No age bunch was saved, as the skeletons of adolescents, youthful grown-ups and middle-age people were found inside the house. The archeological site is currently called "Hamin-Mangha" and is outstanding amongst other saved prehistoric locales in northeastern China. Archeological and anthropological examination demonstrates that the epidemic happened rapidly enough that there was no time for appropriate internments, and the site was not occupied once more.

PLAGUE OF ATHENS (430 B.C.)

Around 430 B.C., not long after a war among Athens and Sparta started, an epidemic attacked the people of Athens and went on for five years. A few appraisals put the loss of life as high as 100,000 people. The Greek student of history Thucydides (460-400 B.C.) composed that "people healthy were out of nowhere assaulted by savage warms in the head, and redness and aggravation in the eyes, the inward parts, for example, the throat or tongue, getting ridiculous and transmitting an unnatural and rank breath" (interpretation by Richard Crawley from the book "The History of the Peloponnesian War," London Dent, 1914).

What precisely this epidemic was has long been a wellspring of discussion among researchers; various ailments have been advanced as potential outcomes, including typhoid, fever and Ebola. Numerous researchers accept that congestion brought about by the war exacerbated the epidemic. Sparta's military was more grounded, driving the Athenians to take asylum behind a progression of fortresses called the "long dividers" that secured their city. Regardless of the epidemic, the war progressed forward, holding off on consummation until 404 B.C., when Athens had to cede to Sparta.

ANTONINE PLAGUE (165-180) A.D.

When troopers came back to the Roman Empire from battling, they brought back more than the riches of triumph. The Antonine Plague, which may have been smallpox, ruined to the military and may have slaughtered more than 5 million individuals in the Roman empire, composed April Pudsey, a senior speaker in Roman History at Manchester Metropolitan University, in a paper distributed in the book "Incapacity in Antiquity," Routledge, 2017).

Numerous history specialists accept that the plague was first brought into the Roman Empire by officers getting back after a war against Parthia. The scourge added as far as possible of the Pax Romana (the Roman Peace), a period from 27 B.C. to A.D. 180, when Rome was at the tallness of its capacity. After A.D. 180, unsteadiness developed all through the Roman Empire, as it encountered increasingly considerate wars and attacks by "savage gatherings. Christianity turned out to be progressively well known in the time after the plague happened.

PLAGUE OF JUSTINIAN (541-542 A.D.)

The Byzantine Empire was desolated by the bubonic plague, which denoted the beginning of its decrease. The plague re-occurred intermittently afterward. A few evaluations suggest that up to 10% of the total populace passed on.

The plague is named after the Byzantine Emperor Justinian (A.D. 527-565). Under his rule, the Byzantine empire arrived at its most prominent degree, controlling region that extended from the Middle East to Western Europe. Justinian developed an incredible basilica known as hagia-sophia ("Holy Wisdom") in Constantinople (cutting edge Istanbul), the empire's capital. Justinian additionally became ill with the plague and endure; be that as it may, his empire progressively lost region in the time after the plague struck.

THE BLACK DEATH (1346-1353)

The Black passing went from Asia to Europe, leaving demolition afterward. A few appraisals suggest that it cleared out over portion of Europe's populace. It was brought about by a strain of the bacterium Yersinia pestis that is likely wiped out today and was spread by insects on contaminated rodents. The assemblages of casualties were covered in mass graves.

The plague changed the course of Europe's history. With such a significant number of dead, work got more diligently to discover, achieving better compensation for laborers and the finish of Europe's arrangement of serfdom. Studies suggest that enduring laborers would be advised to access to meat and greater bread. The absence of modest work may likewise have added to mechanical development.

AMERICAN PLAGUE (SIXTEENTH CENTURY)

The American Plagues are a group of Eurasian infections brought to the Americas by European adventurers. These diseases, including smallpox, added to the breakdown of the Inca and Aztec human advancements. A few appraisals propose that 90% of the indigenous population in the Western Hemisphere was killed off.

The sicknesses helped a Spanish power led by Heman cortes vanquish the Aztec capital of Tenochititlan in 1519 and another Spanish power led by Francisco Pizarro overcome the Incas in 1532. The Spanish assumed control over the regions of the two realms. In the two cases, the Aztec and Incan armed forces had been desolated by illness and couldn't withstand the Spanish powers. At the point when residents of Britain, France, Portugal and the Netherlands started investigating, overcoming and settling the Western Hemisphere, they were additionally helped by the way that malady had endlessly diminished the size of any indigenous gatherings that contradicted them

GREAT PLAGUE OF LONDON (1665-1666)

The Black Death's last significant episode in Great Britain caused a mass migration from London, led by King Charles II. The plague started in April 1665 and spread quickly through the blistering summer months. Insects from plague-tainted rodents were one of the fundamental driver of transmission. When the plague finished, around 100,000 individuals, including 15% of the population of London, had passed on. In any case, this was not the finish of that city's torment. On Sept. 2, 1666, the Great Fire of London started, going on for four days and torching an enormous part of the city.

GREAT PLAGUEOF MARSEILLE (1720-1723)

Authentic records state that the Great Plague of Marseille started when a boat called Grand-Saint-Antoine docked in Marseille, France, conveying a load of products from the eastern Mediterranean. Despite the fact that the boat was isolated, plague despite everything got into the city, likely through bugs on plague-tainted rodents.

Plague spread rapidly, and throughout the following three years, upwards of 100,000 individuals may have kicked the bucket in Marseille and encompassing territories. It's assessed that up to 30% of the population of Marseille may have died.

RUSSIAN PLAGUE (1770-1772)

In plague-attacked Moscow, the dread of isolated residents emitted into savagery. Uproars spread through the city and finished in the homicide of Archbishop Ambrosius, who was urging swarms not to accumulate for venerate.

The ruler of Russia, Catherine II (additionally called Catherine the great), was so edgy to contain the plague and reestablish open request that she gave a rushed announcement requesting that all production lines be moved from Moscow. When the plague finished, upwards of 100,000 individuals may have passed on. Significantly after the plague finished, Catherine struggled to reestablish request. In 1773, YemelyanPugachev, a man who professed to be Peter III (Catherine's executed spouse), led an uprising that brought about the passings of thousands more.

PHILADELPHIA YELLOW FEVER EPIDEMIC (1793)

At the point when yellow fever held onto Philadelphia, the United States' capital at that point, authorities wrongly accepted that slaves were insusceptible. Therefore, abolitionists called for people of African starting point to be selected to nurture the wiped out.

The disease is conveyed and transmitted by mosquitoes, which encountered a populace blast during the especially blistering and damp summer climate in Philadelphia that year. It wasn't until winter shown up — and the mosquitoes ceased to exist — that the epidemic at long last halted. By at that point, in excess of 5,000 people had passed on.

FLU PANDEMIC (1889-1890)

In the cutting edge mechanical age, new vehicle joins made it simpler for influenza infections to unleash ruin. In only a couple of months, the disease crossed the globe, killing 1 million people. It took only five weeks for the epidemic to arrive at top mortality.

The most punctual cases were accounted for in Russia. The infection spread quickly all through St. Petersburg before it immediately advanced all through Europe and the remainder of the world, in spite of the way that air travel didn't exist yet

AMERICAN POLIO EPIDEMIC (1916)

A polio epidemic that began in New York City caused 27,000 cases and 6,000 passings in the United States. The disease essentially influences youngsters and some of the time leaves survivors with changeless incapacities.

Polio epidemics happened sporadically in the United States until the Salk immunization was created in 1954. As the antibody turned out to be broadly accessible, cases in the United States declined. The last polio case in the United States was accounted for in 1979. Overall immunization endeavors have enormously diminished the disease, in spite of the fact that it isn't yet totally killed

SPANISH FLU (1918-1920)

An expected 500 million people from the South Seas toward the North Pole succumbed to Spanish Flu. One-fifth of those kicked the bucket, with some indigenous networks pushed to the verge of elimination. The flu's spread and lethality was upgraded by the confined states of officers and poor wartime sustenance that numerous people were encountering during World War I.

In spite of the name Spanish Flu, the disease likely didn't begin in Spain. Spain was an impartial country during the war and didn't uphold severe restriction of its press, which could along these lines unreservedly distribute early records of the disease. Subsequently, people erroneously accepted the ailment was explicit to Spain, and the name Spanish Flu stuck.

ASIAN FLU (1957-58)

The Asian Flu pandemic was another worldwide appearing for influenza. With its underlying foundations in China, the disease asserted more than 1 million lives. The infection that caused the pandemic was a mix of avian flu infections.

The places for disease and control contamination takes note of that the disease spread quickly and was accounted for in Singapore in February 1957, Hong Kong in April 1957, and the beach front urban areas of the United States in the mid year of 1957. The all out loss of life was more than 1.1 million around the world, with 116,000 passings happening in the United States.

AIDS (1981- TILL PRESENT)

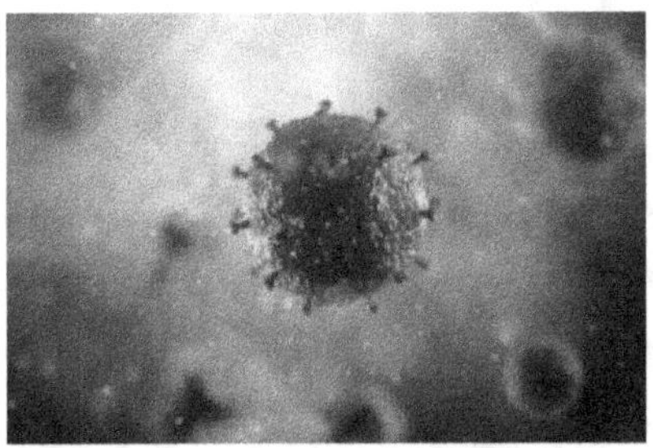

Helps has guaranteed an expected 35 million lives since it was first distinguished. HIV, which is the virus that causes AIDS, likely created from a chimpanzee virus that moved to people in West Africa during the 1920s. The virus advanced far and wide, and AIDS was a pandemic by the late twentieth century. Presently, about 64% of the assessed 40 million living with Human Immunodeficiency virus (HIV) live in sub-Saharan Africa.

For a considerable length of time, the disease had no known fix, however medicine created during the 1990s currently permits people with the disease to encounter an ordinary life expectancy with standard treatment. Considerably all the more promising, two people have been Cured of HIV starting at mid 2020

H1N1 SWINE FLU (2009-10)

The 2009 swine flu pandemic was brought about by another strain of H1N1 that started in Mexico in the spring of 2009 preceding spreading to the remainder of the world. In one year, the virus contaminated the same number of as 1.4 billion people over the globe and murdered somewhere in the range of 151,700 and 575,400 people.

The 2009 flu pandemic fundamentally influenced youngsters and youthful grown-ups, and 80% of the deaths were in people more youthful than 65, the CDC reported. That was bizarre, taking into account that most strains of flu viruses, including those that cause regular flu, cause the most noteworthy level of deaths in people ages 65 and more established. However, on account of the swine flu, more seasoned people appeared to have just developed enough insusceptibility to the gathering of viruses that H1N1 has a place with, so weren't influenced so a lot. An antibody for the H1N1 virus that caused the swine flu is presently remembered for the yearly flu immunization.

WEST AFRICA EBOLA EPIDEMIC (2014-2016)

Ebola desolated West Africa somewhere in the range of 2014 and 2016, with 28,600 reported cases and 11,325 deaths. The primary case to be reported was in Guinea in December 2013, at that point the disease immediately spread to Liberia and Sierra Leone. The greater part of the cases and deaths happened in those three nations. Fewer cases happened in Nigeria, Mali, Senegal, the United States and Europe, the Centers for Disease Control and Prevention Reported.

There is no remedy for Ebola, in spite of the fact that endeavors at finding an immunization are continuous. The principal known instances of Ebola happened in Sudan and the Democratic Republic of Congo in 1976, and the virus may have begun in bats.

NOVEL CORONA VIRUS (COVID 19) 2020

As Novel Corona Virus (covid-19) episode of Pneumonia in Wuhan, China in December 2019. It most likely originate from wet markets in china.Covid-19 are a class of viruses that are single strand of RNA. They are commonly four diverse subtypes of these viruses:

1. Alpha corona virus

2. Beta corona virus

3. Delta corona virus

4. Gamma corona virus

These viruses have their envelope and the case defenseless to cleansers. Do wash your hands and routinely to be extraordinary useful as far as disposing of the viruses.

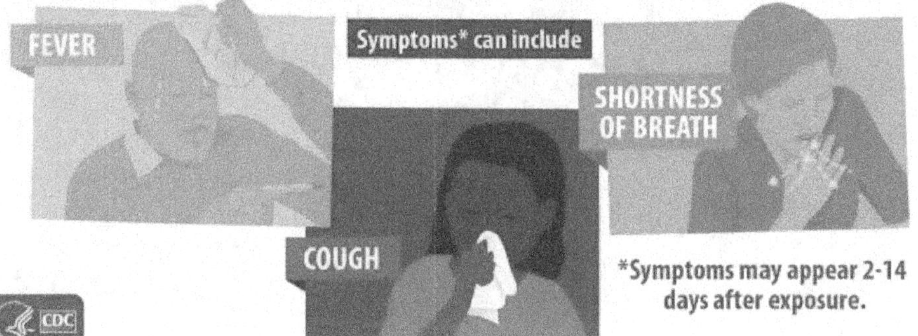

SYMPTOMS OF CORONAVIRUS DISEASE 2019
Patients with COVID-19 have experienced mild to severe respiratory illness.
FEVER
Symptoms* can include
SHORTNESS OF BREATH
COUGH
*Symptoms may appear 2-14 days after exposure.
CDC

Covid-19 is very much a disease of the moment, emerging in a crowded city in a newly prosperous and connected China before spreading to the rest of the world in a matter of months. But our response to it has been both hyper-modern and practically medieval. Scientists around the world are using cutting-edge tools to rapidly sequence the genome of the coronavirus, pass along information about its virulence, and collaborate on possible countermeasures and vaccines, all far quicker than could have been done before.

But when the virus arrived among us, our only effective response was to shut down society and turn off the assembly line of global capitalism. Minus the text alerts, the videoconferencing and the Netflix, what we were doing wasn't that different from what our ancestors might have tried to halt an outbreak of the plague. The result has been chemotherapy for the global economy.

Just as the eventual emergence of something like Covid-19 was easily predictable, so too are the actions we should have taken to shore ourselves against its coming.

We need to strengthen the global health, to ensure that when the next virus emerges — which it will — we'll catch it faster, perhaps even snuff it out. The budget of the WHO, the agency ostensibly charged with safeguarding the health of the world's 7.8 billion citizens in the U.S.

We need to double down on the development of vaccines, which will include assuring large pharma companies that their investments won't be wasted should an outbreak end before one is ready.

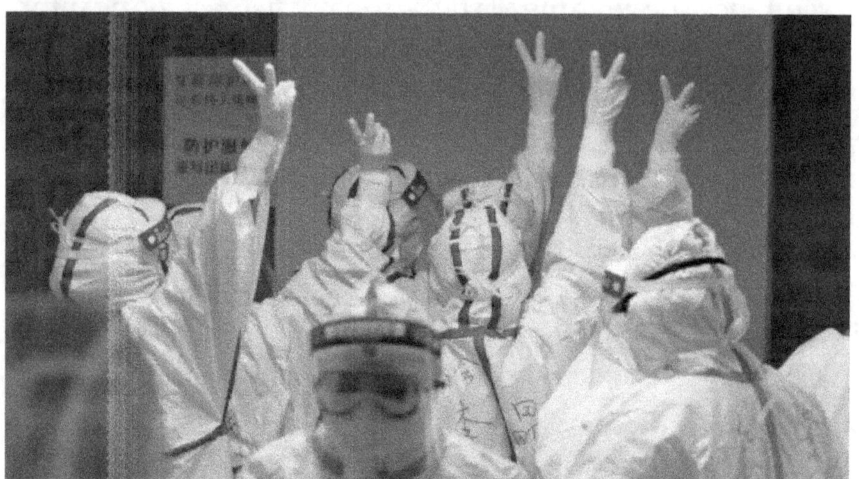

We need to build more slack into our public health systems. Just as the US military is designed — and funded — to fight a war on two fronts, so our health care systems should have the surge capacity to meet the next pandemic.

One ongoing challenge in pandemic preparation is what experts call shock and forgetting. Too often politicians make funding promises in the immediate aftermath of a crisis like Sars or Ebola, only to let those pledges lapse as the memory of the outbreak fades.

Somehow, I expect that won't be the case with Covid-19. We need to do all we can to not just survive this pandemic, but to ensure it remains a throwback from the past, not a sign of things to come.

www.ingramcontent.com/pod-product-compliance
Lightning Source LLC
Chambersburg PA
CBHW070329160726
47999CB00003B/1221